Animals Growing Up™

How Lions Grow Up

Lisa Idzikowski

Enslow Publishing
101 W. 23rd Street
Suite 240
New York, NY 10011
USA
enslow.com

WORDS TO KNOW

ambush To lie in wait, then pounce.

carnivore An animal that eats meat.

coalition A small group of male lions.

crèche A lion family nursery.

cub A baby lion.

lioness A female lion.

pride A family of lions.

sibling A brother or sister.

social Living together in groups.

territory A large area of land where lions live.

CONTENTS

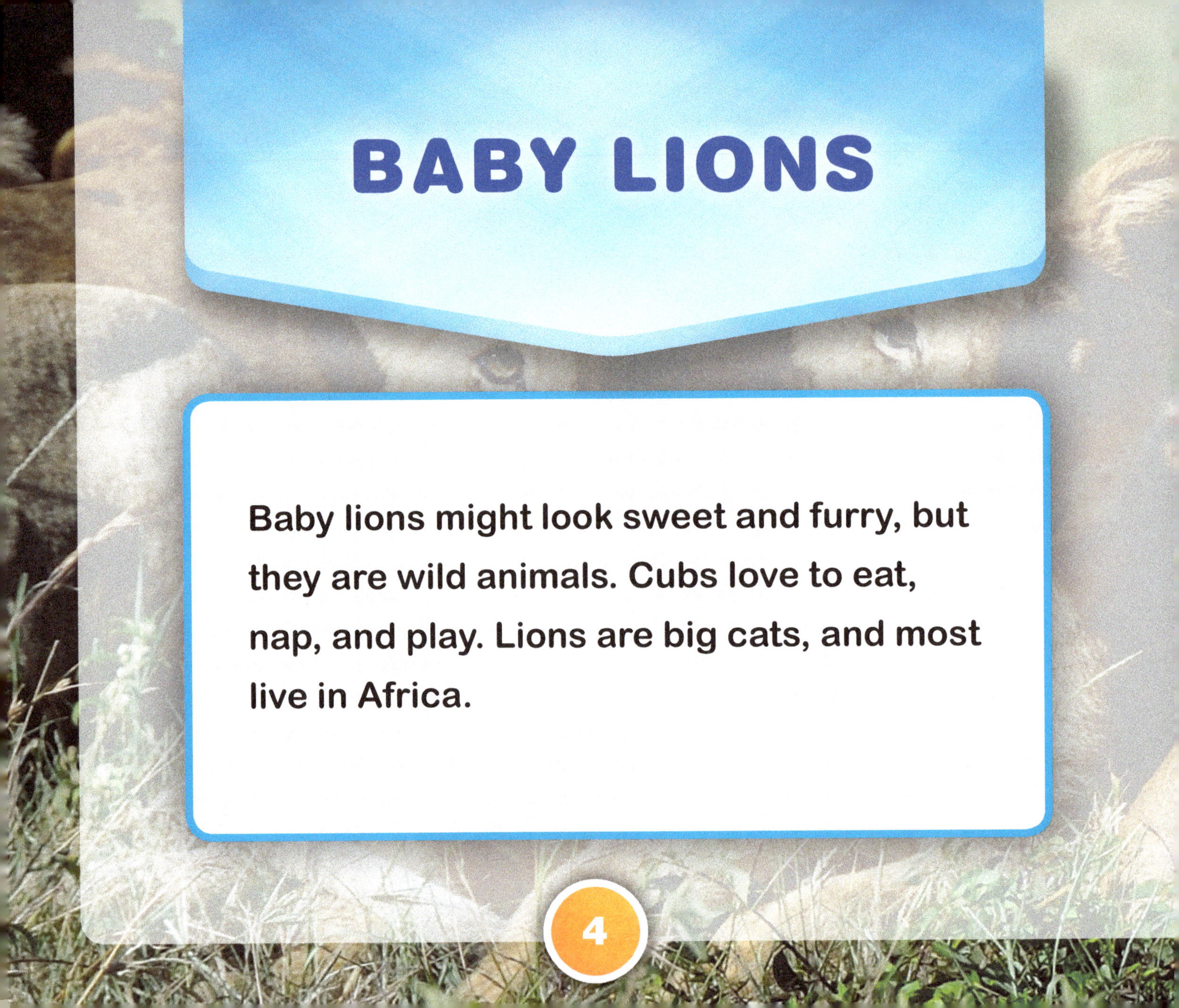

BABY LIONS

Baby lions might look sweet and furry, but they are wild animals. Cubs love to eat, nap, and play. Lions are big cats, and most live in Africa.

FAST FACT

A baby lion is called a **cub**.

Two young lion cubs cuddle together.

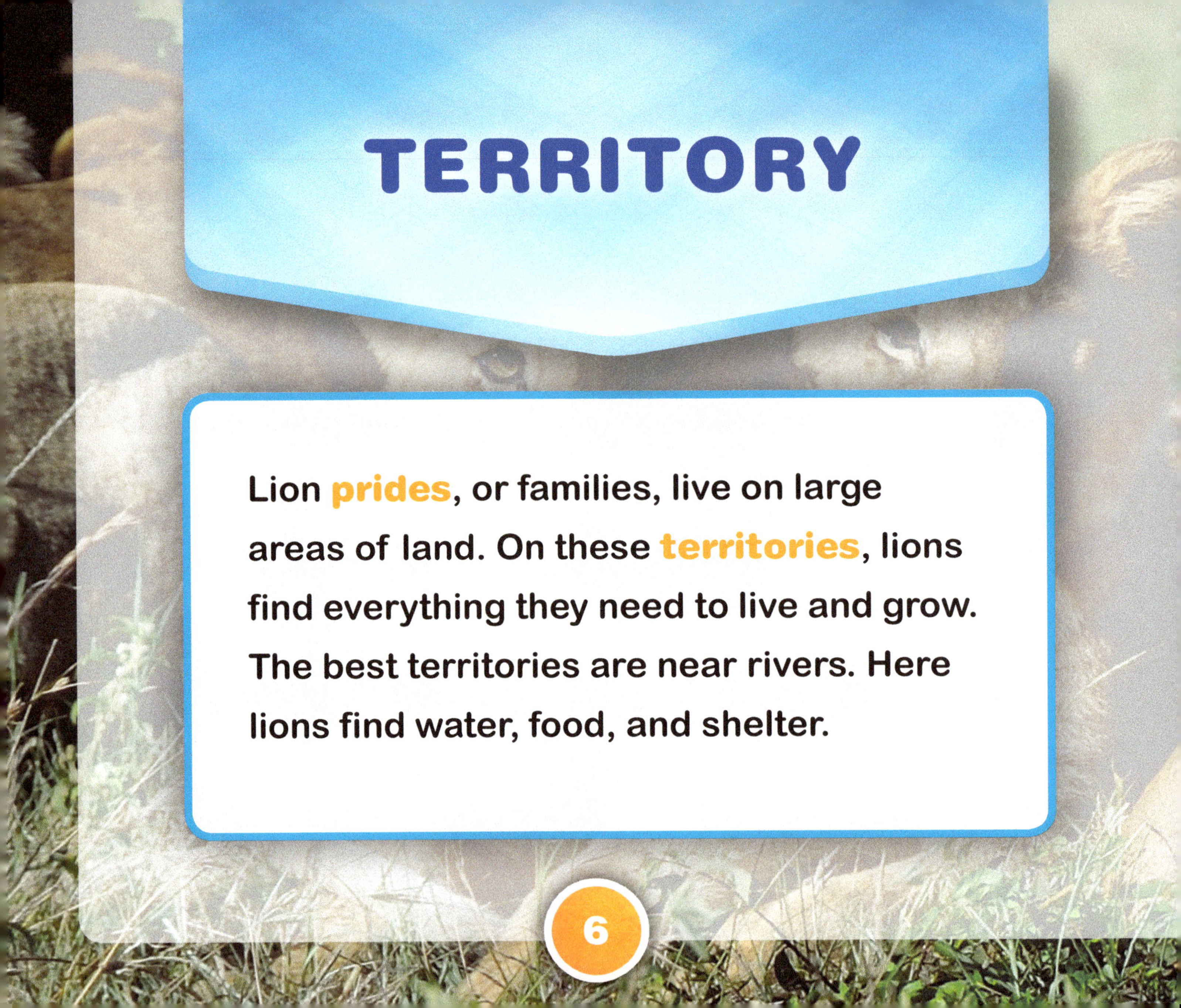

TERRITORY

Lion **prides**, or families, live on large areas of land. On these **territories**, lions find everything they need to live and grow. The best territories are near rivers. Here lions find water, food, and shelter.

A pride watches over its territory.

FAST FACT

Lions spend more time sleeping than any other African animal.

CUBS ARE BORN

A **lioness** must find a safe place to have her cubs. When her cubs are born, they cannot see. They cannot walk. She must care for them completely.

FAST FACT

Lion cubs are between about 2½ and 4½ pounds (1 and 2 kilograms) when born.

A newborn cub calls out for his mother.

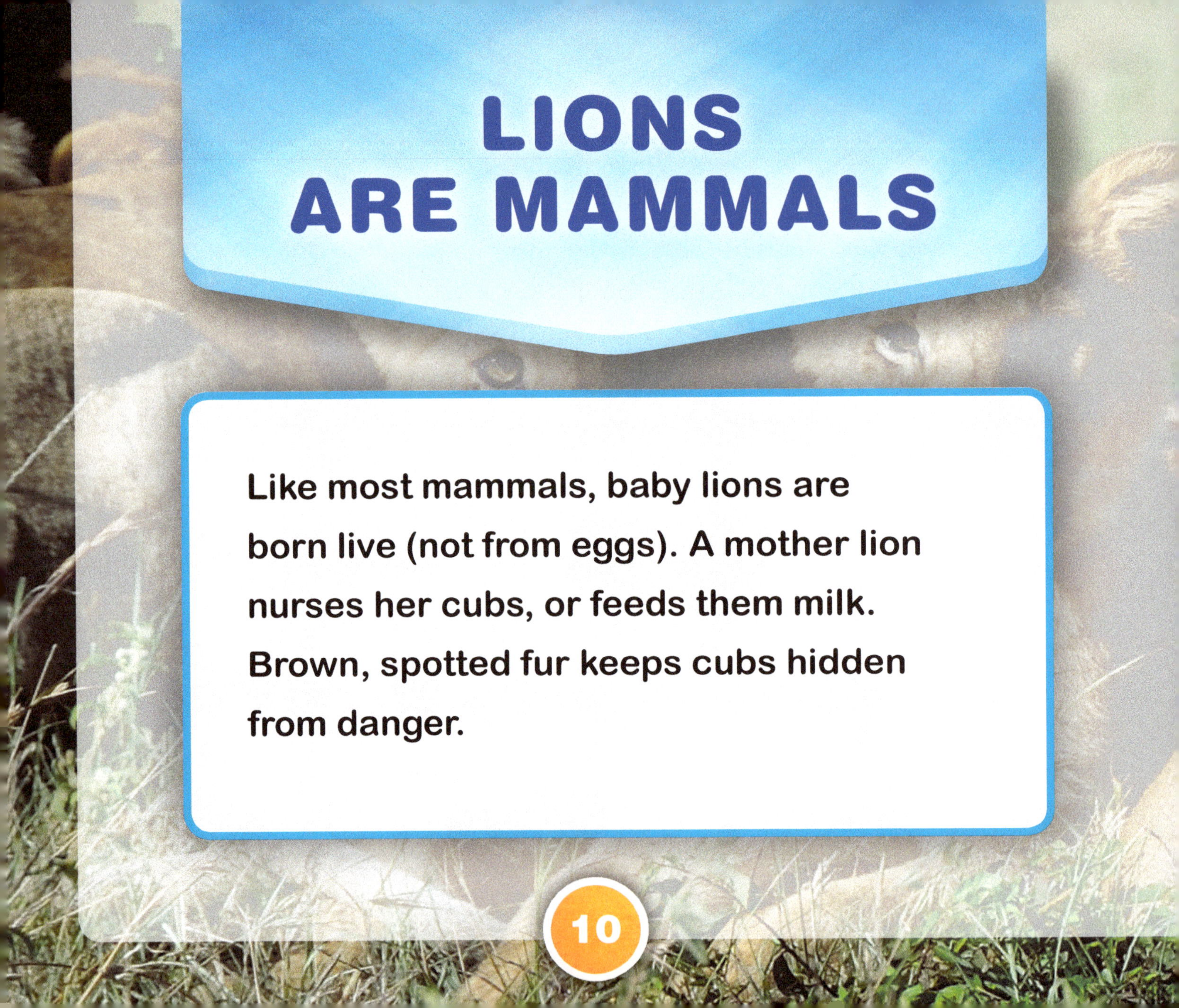

LIONS ARE MAMMALS

Like most mammals, baby lions are born live (not from eggs). A mother lion nurses her cubs, or feeds them milk. Brown, spotted fur keeps cubs hidden from danger.

FAST FACT

Lion cubs only eat or drink their mother's milk until they're about six weeks old.

A lioness nurses her spotted cubs.

SOCIAL ANIMALS

Lions are **social** animals. Mothers, grandmothers, sisters, aunts, and several male lions live together in a pride. At about six weeks old, cubs move to the family nursery.

FAST FACT

A **coalition** is a small group of male lions that belongs to a pride.

A male lion, lioness, and two cubs from a pride rest together.

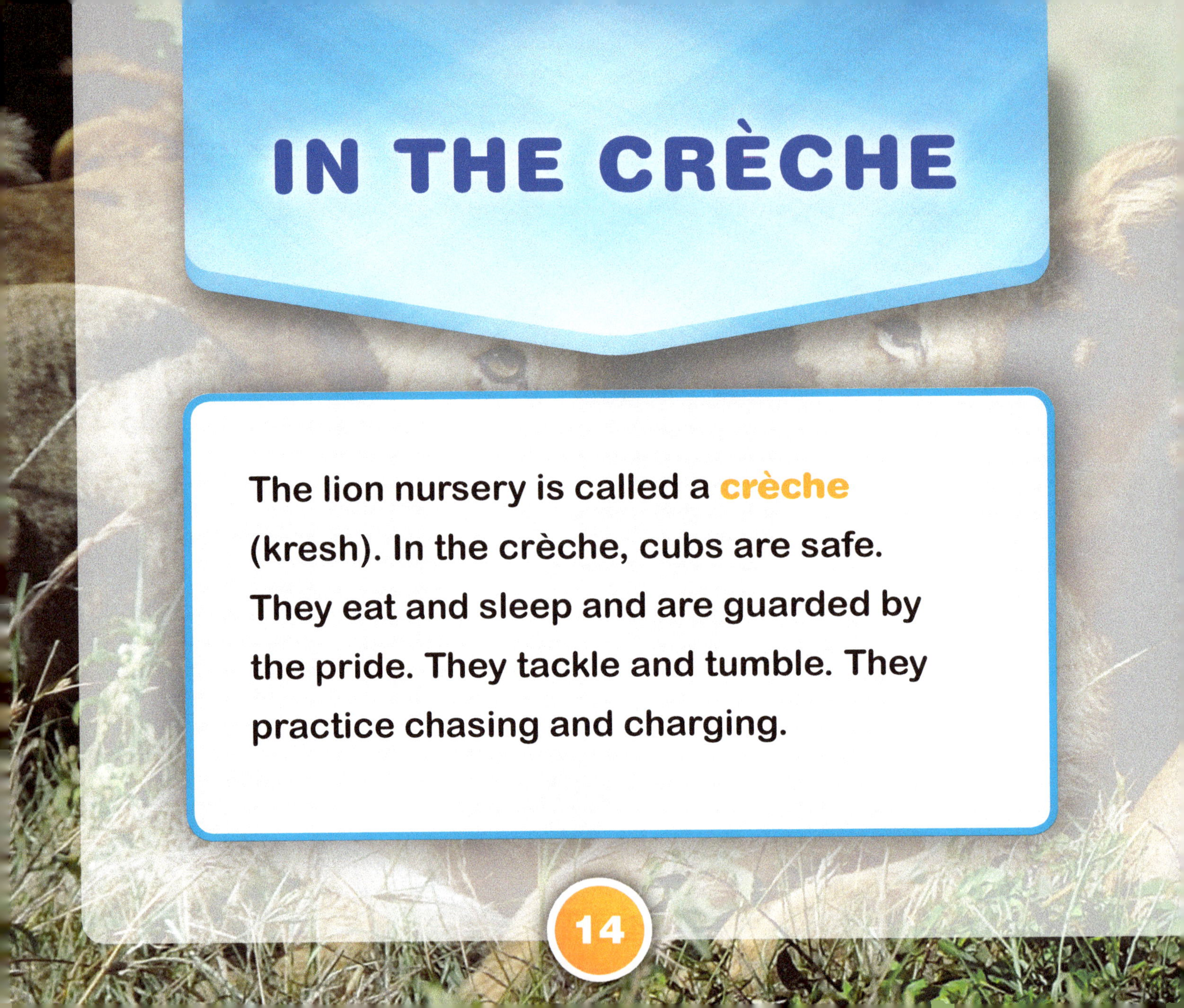

IN THE CRÈCHE

The lion nursery is called a **crèche** (kresh). In the crèche, cubs are safe. They eat and sleep and are guarded by the pride. They tackle and tumble. They practice chasing and charging.

FAST FACT

After about three months, cubs begin to eat meat. After six months, they eat only meat.

Cubs play-fight to practice for life in the wild.

WHAT'S FOR DINNER?

Lions are **carnivores**, or meat eaters. They **ambush** their prey. A lone lioness hunts small animals, such as warthogs. Several lionesses together might attack a zebra. Males capture the largest animals, such as buffalo or giraffes.

FAST FACT

Sometimes lions eat so much, they won't eat again for about a week!

A lioness captures an antelope to eat.

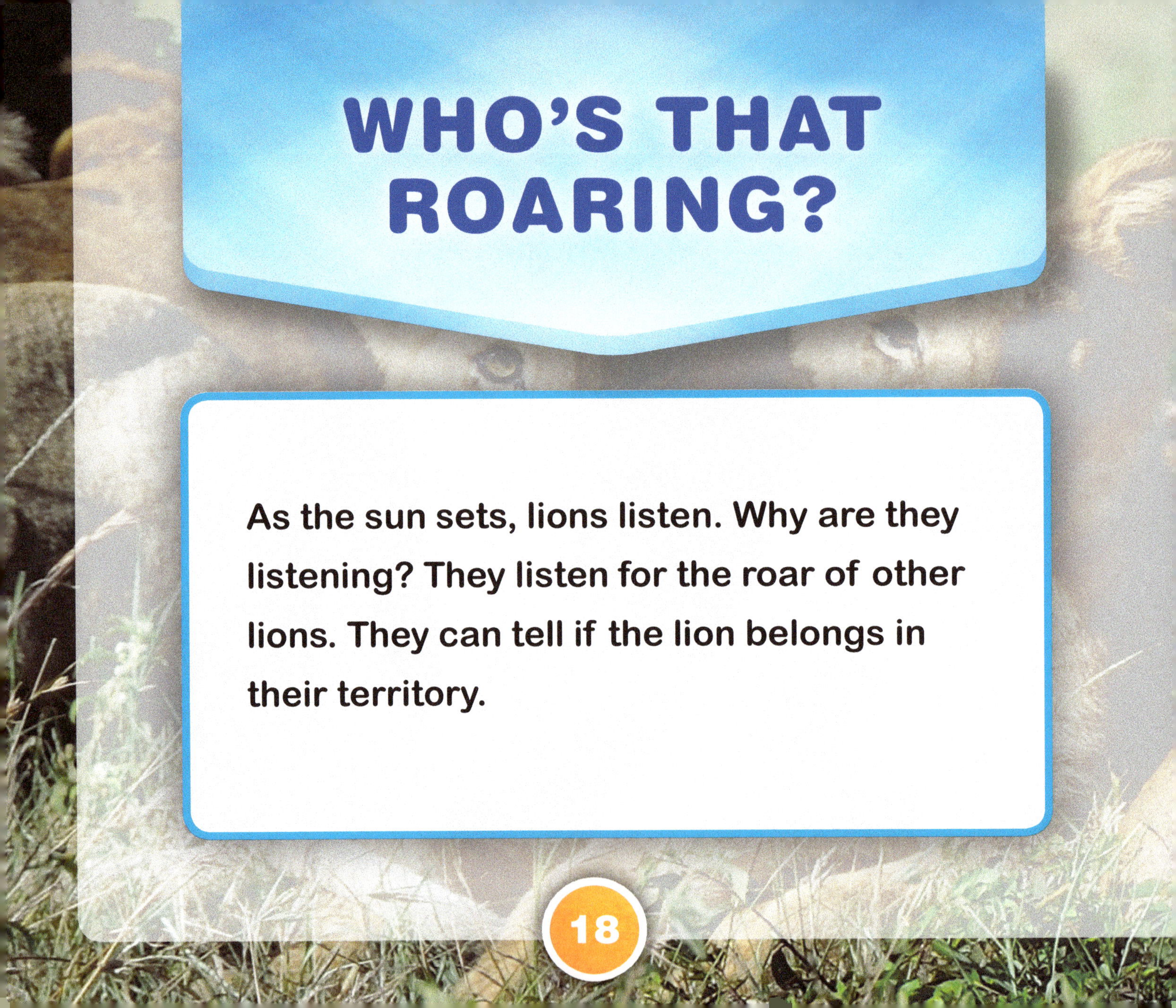

WHO'S THAT ROARING?

As the sun sets, lions listen. Why are they listening? They listen for the roar of other lions. They can tell if the lion belongs in their territory.

A cub listens as a male roars. He warns other lions to stay away.

FAST FACT

Lions usually roar between dusk and dawn.

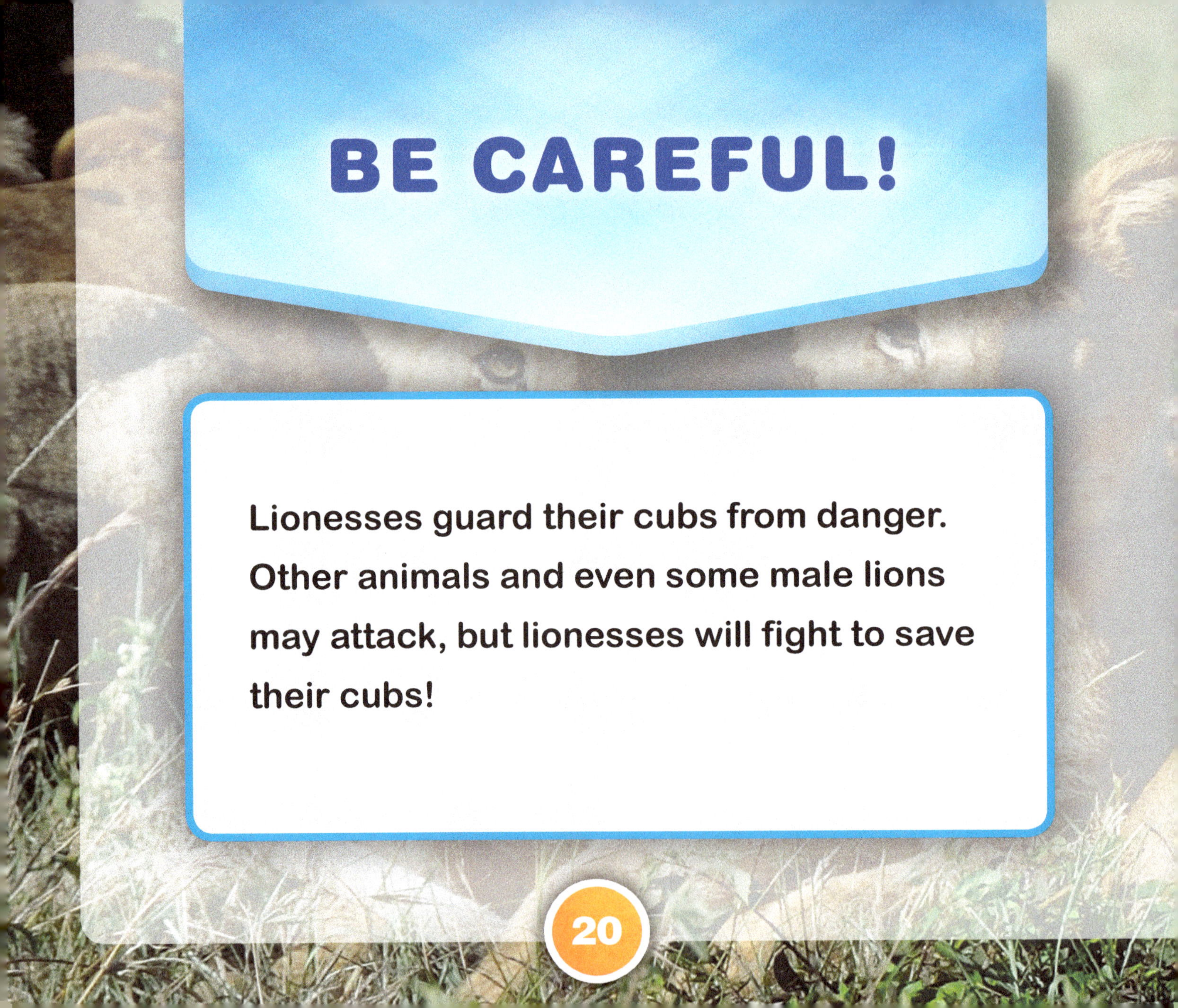

BE CAREFUL!

Lionesses guard their cubs from danger. Other animals and even some male lions may attack, but lionesses will fight to save their cubs!

FAST FACT

The biggest threats to lions are people moving onto their lands.

A lioness will fight any animal that tries to hurt her cubs.

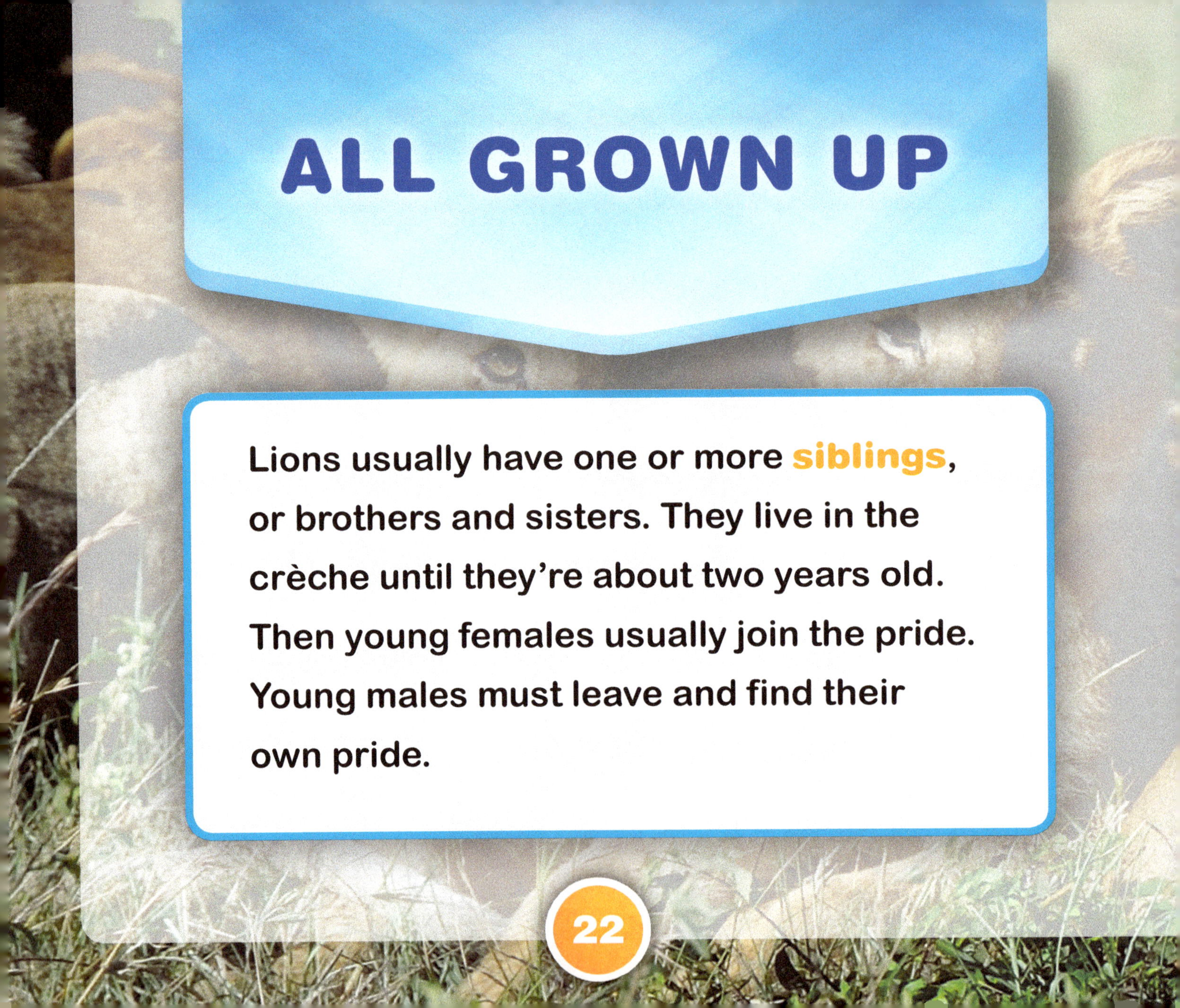

ALL GROWN UP

Lions usually have one or more **siblings**, or brothers and sisters. They live in the crèche until they're about two years old. Then young females usually join the pride. Young males must leave and find their own pride.

A young male is ready to be on his own.

FAST FACT

Males have thick, fluffy manes around their heads and necks. Females do not.

LEARN MORE

Books

Klepeis, Alicia Z. *Lions on the Hunt*. Minneapolis, MN: Lerner Classroom, 2017.

Koster, Amy Sky. *Lions*. Washington, DC: National Geographic Children's Books, 2018.

Marsh, Laura. *Lions*. Washington, DC: National Geographic Children's Books, 2015.

Websites

National Geographic Kids: Lion
kids.nationalgeographic.com/animals/lion/#ww-wild-cats-lion.jpg
Learn all about lions.

San Diego Zoo Kids: African Lion
kids.sandiegozoo.org/animals/african-lion
Read fun facts about a lion's life in the wild.

INDEX

Published in 2019 by Enslow Publishing, LLC.
101 W. 23rd Street, Suite 240, New York, NY 10011

Library of Congress Cataloging-in-Publication Data

Names: Idzikowski, Lisa, author.
Title: How lions grow up / Lisa Idzikowski.
Description: New York, NY : Enslow Publishing, 2019. | Series: Animals growing up | Includes bibliographical references and index. | Audience: Grades K to 3.
Identifiers: LCCN 2017045220| ISBN 9780766096516 (library bound) | ISBN 9780766096523 (pbk.) | ISBN 9780766096530 (6 pack)
Subjects: LCSH: Lion—Development—Juvenile literature. | Lion—Infancy—Juvenile literature.
Classification: LCC QL737.C23 I39 2017 | DDC 599.7571/392—dc23
LC record available at https://lccn.loc.gov/2017045220

Printed in the United States of America

Photos Credits: Cover, p. 1 Franz Aberham/The Image Bank/Getty Images; pp. 4–23 (background image), 7 (main photo) Volodymyr Burdiak/Shutterstock.com; p. 5 Theodore Mattas/Shutterstock.com; p. 9 Jean-Michel Labat/Science Source; p. 11 © webguzs/iStock/Thinkstock; p. 13 © dv029069/Photodisc/Thinkstock; p. 15 Maggy Meyer/Shutterstock.com; p. 17 Bildagentur Zoonar GmbH/Shutterstock.com; p. 19 Steve Wiechman/Shutterstock.com; p. 21 Gudkov Andrey/Shutterstock.com; p. 23 Four Oaks/Shutterstock.com.